Stoners in America

Stoners in America

AMERICANS SMOKING MARIJUANA REGULARLY

Jose Carranza M.D. and Octavio Carranza B.S.

Contents

Preface

Why are we writing this book?

I am a practicing psychiatrist and have been for over thirty years. In my practice I have seen the devastation induced by marijuana smoking in America.

My son, Octavio, who has a bachelor's degree in medicine, has helped me to look for scientific papers on marijuana and its effects on the brain and other organs.

I have been shocked by the large number of people addicted to marijuana and by the continuous false rumors about marijuana smoking, such as "It's a great pastime," "It is only recreational," "It is better to smoke pot than drink alcoholic beverages," "Marijuana is not addicting," "Marijuana is a medicine," and so on.

So, as a conscientious physician, I am shocked to see the massive number of Americans addicted to marijuana who are not aware that this is *a disease*.

I am not a "moralizer." I do not try to tell people what to do with their lives. I just want every American to be aware that smoking marijuana is an *illness*, an *addiction*, and as such should be prevented. If you are already a marijuana smoker, please consider that *total sobriety*, or quitting smoking marijuana, is a very important option in your life, and after trying for a period of at least six months *not smoking marijuana at all*, then you have the real option of freedom to decide if you want to continue smoking it.

Quit smoking it and become introspective, and you will realize that without smoking marijuana you will have a clear mind and no memory problems.

If you are a stoner already, think also if you want your children to learn that smoking marijuana is okay, because you know children learn behaviors from their parents.

Also, on an international perspective, as a "stoner" you should know that the United States of America is no longer the number one country in our economy. We are the most powerful military power in the world, and you have contributed to making the United States the "champion" of marijuana smoking!

CHAPTER 1

The "Stoners," or Marijuana-Smoking Americans

American people who smoke marijuana regularly believe it is a safe recreational pastime. "Stoners" believe it is harmless, and they also believe it is a medicine that can help people in the treatment of several conditions.

Pot smokers believe marijuana smoking should be legal and that anyone smoking it should not be considered a criminal and thus never be incarcerated for smoking it or for its possession. Stoners believe you should make your own decision that smoking marijuana is safe, and that you do not have to ask any physician if it is harmful for them or their children. Many stoners have been smoking pot for over twenty years, and they really believe they've never had a problem.

Stoners believe that if they decide to quit smoking pot, it is their own personal decision, and it should not be a physician recommendation. However, stoners should know that it is about time to learn more about the real effects of marijuana on the brain, heart, and lungs. So, without prejudice, I want you to read all about the effects of marijuana. This is the reason I am writing this book. In this book you'll learn about the following:

- The chemistry of marijuana and the pollution it causes in your brain
- If marijuana smoking is what is producing your memory impairment
- If marijuana smoking is affecting your fertility
- If marijuana is truly a medicine, since it is sold in many dispensaries, or if it is only a business for the new drug dealers, also called dispensaries
- If you are really a drug addict, as with heroin, amphetamine, and cocaine addicts
- If you can quit by yourself whenever you want to without any problem
- Why alcohol drinking is legal and marijuana smoking is illegal
- If it is safe to smoke marijuana while you are pregnant
- If you have to tell your family doctor that you smoke marijuana regularly
- If you can be considered a mental patient, since the American Psychiatric Association has labeled you "marijuana-dependent," which is a mental illness
- If marijuana smoking will interfere with your driving
- If marijuana intoxication will make you more isolated and less aggressive
- Why the many mass murders occurring in America, such as at "Columbine"; the shooter at a theater in Colorado; the shooting in Tucson, Arizona; the young man who killed his mother and then killed many children in Connecticut; the student who killed several people in a campus in West Virginia; the guy who killed several people in a church in South Carolina; more recently the mass murder at a junior college in Oregon; and the man who killed his wife and child and then killed himself—why were all these perpetrators marijuana addicts?

CHAPTER 2

Marijuana Addiction

I t was in the sixties when Americans really began smoking marijuana and using many other illegal drugs as a protest against the Establishment and against the American government of President Nixon and Secretary Kissinger, who were very active in promoting the military intervention of America in Vietnam. Marijuana smoking had never been a cultural use of an intoxicant in America, so it should be considered an *epidemic*, or a use of a foreign drug in the Americas. The only "cultural" intoxicant in America, as in many of our ancestors' European countries, has been alcohol (wine, beer, and liquor), and tobacco was smoked by Native Americans.

So this addiction or massive epidemic began as our young people demonstrated against the Vietnam War. Thousands, if not millions, were refusing to go to that war. Many left the country and remained in Canada, Mexico, or Europe. Young Americans were not so wrong in their opposition to the Vietnam War. It was considered by many to be a genocide.

The immorality of the Vietnam War was clearly shown by the military personnel who already had been there and also became activists against the war in Vietnam. These demonstrations happened all over the United States. Student riots in many universities even resulted in the death of some college students. The famous Woodstock Festival in New York State is a good example of an antiwar demonstration where thousands of young people got together to protest the war, and while doing this, they also became addicted to marijuana and many other illegal drugs.

Then Americans soon learned that marijuana grew anywhere, and it became easily accessible, although since the beginning of the twentieth century, it has always been a business for drug dealers.

In many surveys, it has been calculated that over twenty million Americans are regular smokers of marijuana, and since the legal amendments in Colorado and Washington, this number might now be over twenty-five million Americans smoking marijuana—daily, weekly, monthly, or whenever they are offered "joints" by their friends.

When a disease spreads so much is when in medicine we call it an epidemic, and yes, we have a marijuana addiction epidemic in America now.

One of the main characteristics of drug addiction is that an addict does not recognize the use of his or her drug as an addiction. Addicts just keep using it and have plenty of excuses. In the case of marijuana, they say, "marijuana is not as bad as alcohol," or "it is just a pastime," and because it has so spread that it is shown in movies as "normal," some people use the excuse that "it is part of the American culture." But marijuana and hashish are not part of the American culture or civilization at all.

Marijuana and the more powerful hashish had been used culturally only in the Muslim Arab countries and in India. Actually, the word *hashish* is a derivative of *hashishin*—or *assassin*—since the Arabs for centuries used hashish to intoxicate people that they sent to kill someone. Like marijuana, it numbed their feelings so they could easily commit murders. And maybe this is the same mechanism behind why the mass murders in America have happened. The criminals were smoking marijuana, and either they became psychotic, or they were only numbing their feelings and went on to kill many people.

In my experience in Mexico, the Mexican government also used marijuana intoxication, giving it to military people when they were sent to murder groups of people or families who were trying to change Mexico into a democracy. They had whole troops intoxicated, and only the drivers of the military trucks were not smoking, so when the troops got to the place where they had to murder men, women, and children, they felt numbed by the marijuana they had been smoking for twenty-four hours of more prior to their actions.

But culturally, marijuana has never been part of American civilization nor of the Mexican culture.

The only drug used for centuries by Native Americans was tobacco, which is still grown in America too and has been commercialized. Legal nicotine is also addicting, but in small doses it is a mild stimulant. The main health problem with smoking cigarettes and marijuana joints in large quantities is that, around age twenty-five or thirty, a person's lung cells become more sensitive to the carcinogenic effects of these two "smokes."

At the time when the English and Spaniards invaded the Americas, they used marijuana for hemp only. It was helpful as a fiber in their ships, but Europeans never smoked marijuana nor hashish.

The marijuana epidemic began in this country in the sixties. Even in Mexico, people began to smoke it in the Mexican Revolution of 1910–1917, never before. Native Mexicans also used alcohol as an intoxicant, as did Europeans at that time. The epidemic of marijuana in Mexico and European countries happened as followers of the young Americans who were opposed to the Vietnam War began smoking. Again, all this happened in the 1960s. Now America is the champion of the world in marijuana smoking.

In summary, marijuana addiction is a disease as much as heroin addiction or cocaine or amphetamine addiction. It has the same characteristics, also named by the American Psychiatric Association as a *dependence,* meaning the habitual use of it, and a clear sense of *needing to use the drug continuously.* Depending on the joints smoked, this need could be daily, every other day, weekly, or monthly.

It is a very peculiar addiction because there is not a single compound involved as there is in alcohol, heroin, cocaine, or methedrine addictions. In marijuana addiction there is an inhalation of hundreds of chemicals, of which there are at least ten psychotropics and hundreds of terpenes. Terpenes are long-chain hydrocarbons like the ones present in gasoline fumes, glue, or tobacco.

Because of this multiple-chemical addiction, marijuana induces confusion, relaxation, sleepiness, increased appetite or "the munchies," motor impairment, memory lapses, and of course what any stoner would call a state of well-being. Some say it helps them to sleep well; others feel "less depressed." And all this is true. Since each joint smoked is different, the effects of a combination of psychotropics and terpenes has to give very different effects from person to person and from joint to joint.

How is this epidemic transmitted? We know how a viral epidemic is transmitted—by breathing droplets, by touching, by sexual contact—but how is the marijuana epidemic transmitted? It's transmitted by mouth-to-mouth misinformation and by propaganda spread by drug dealers who make millions of dollars selling marijuana, in spite of the so-called "dispensaries." There are also street drug dealers, and of course the so-called "dispensaries" are only legalized drug dealers.

Marijuana smoking and addiction have also spread because of the cinema and mass media in general. There are so many movies made in Hollywood that show Americans smoking marijuana as a normal habit. And we Americans like to watch lots of movies and TV.

As in any addiction, marijuana induces tolerance, and many users after ten years can smoke up to twenty joints per day. Since it is not toxic, and it has even been found that we have cannabinoid receptors in our brains, chronic users believe it is safe.

As with any addiction, there is a withdrawal when discontinued, since marijuana induces both psychological and physical dependence. Unlike heroin and alcohol withdrawal, marijuana withdrawal is not so acute and flagrant. Why? Because of the multichemical addiction of cannabis and the long-acting chemicals and metabolites—some last, attached to the brain, up to three months or more. Alcohol and heroin withdrawals are very acute and dramatic, and they require immediate medical treatment. Marijuana withdrawal does not need medical attention.

Withdrawal of marijuana can appear in two weeks after cessation, and the symptoms are mild. The user just feels "different" or is sleepy or more confused or anxious. Rarely, there are also seizures in the withdrawal of marijuana, and we now have an explanation for that. One of the cannabinoids in marijuana (cannabidiol) has anticonvulsant effects like a barbiturate, so when cessation happens, there might be an isolated seizure.

The millions of Americans who are addicted to marijuana deny it, with allegations (as with any drug or alcohol addict) that they could quit anytime they want to, but they do not want to quit. This is always considered a lie common to all drug and alcohol addicts. They keep using their favorite drug and are dependent or addicted.

Marijuana induces both psychological dependence as well as physical dependence. The latter means that whenever they quit smoking for several weeks, they start having withdrawal symptoms. Marijuana withdrawal could start as late as three weeks after cessation of smoking, since it has four hundred chemical compounds, and the ten to twelve psychotropics are very long-acting, withdrawal symptoms do not emerge in a few days or hours as in alcohol or heroin dependence. It can take weeks before the person starts noticing many behavioral changes, and of course the most common phenomenon is that he or she goes back smoking it, to stop the withdrawal symptoms. But these symptoms are not as dramatic as the ones we see in heroin withdrawal or alcohol withdrawal. They are mild, and users just feel different, anxious, or at times depressed.

However *addiction* is best described now in the APA classification of mental disorders as *dependence*, meaning the habitual smoking of the herb in joints, and a clear sense of need to use the drug. The individual dependent on marijuana might use excuses to continue using it, such as "It helps me sleep," "It increases my appetite," "It works as an antidepressant," and so on. But, again, all these psychological excuses are only a proof of the users' chronic dependence on marijuana.

Withdrawal symptoms are not the only evidence of dependence, and as mentioned before, since marijuana chemicals are such long-acting chemicals in the brain, withdrawal might be mild and can happen over a long period of time.

Being "high" or "stoned" when smoking marijuana causes users to believe that this effect is only happening while they are smoking a new joint. However, we have many publications showing evidence that marijuana chemicals stay bound to brain receptors for months.

If marijuana is an addiction or dependence, should marijuana smokers consider treatment? Marijuana induces both psychological dependence as well as physical dependence. And of course the answer is yes. It can be treated by just the cessation of smoking it. As I said before, it usually takes six months for marijuana smokers to feel different, to think properly, and not to have memory problems. So this is the good news for stoners: if you really quit, you will go back to normal.

CHAPTER 3

Can Marijuana Addiction Be Treated like Any Other Addiction?

Yes, of course. All addictions have the same premises:

- Because of the pleasure involved in its use, addicts feel they do not have an illness, and they do not want to change.
- This addiction, like other drug or alcohol addictions, can cause serious damage to different organs—and eventually death.

So it is highly recommended that marijuana addicts be treated like any other addicts.

Treatment involves, first of all, a desire to be cured, to be healthy. In the case of marijuana, addicts get tired of having memory problems and not functioning well. More recently, it has been recognized that the poor motor coordination marijuana users have under the influence of marijuana has caused many vehicle accidents and deaths.

Treatment of any addiction requires working for oneself with stamina and with a real desire to be sober. Many times is hard, particularly when addicts have been using marijuana for many years, and it has become a part of their life. Their brains cannot recognize what it is to be stoned rather than to be normal. They are always in a daze or confused, and they have forgotten what it is like to be clear-minded. If they are able to work, once they quit marijuana, they will be more productive.

Sleep patterns are altered by marijuana smoking, so that many addicts just want to have a normal night's sleep, even if they began smoking marijuana under the false belief that marijuana would help them to sleep well.

Among the best Treatment Programs are Alcoholics Anonymous, Narcotics Anonymous, and PDAP (Palmer Drug Abuse Program).

Oftentimes the addiction is so chronic that the only good treatments are long-term rehabilitation programs such as Habilitat, located in Honolulu, Hawaii, or Phoenix House in New York and New Jersey. These two programs require a commitment of the addict to stay from eighteen to twenty-four months in rehabilitation. And it makes sense when we realize that if someone has been smoking marijuana for twenty years, it would be impossible to kick the habit in a thirty- to ninety-day program.

The brain of a marijuana-dependent individual gets used to the many chemicals, so a very long period of total sobriety is required before he or she can realize and personally feel different.

I have treated many patients who have been smoking marijuana for two or three years, and I just give them one rule: "Please stop smoking marijuana for six months. Please make that commitment to *yourself*, and then come back to see me." All patients who came back told me how different and clear-minded they felt after six months of sobriety. This, in my long experience in treating drug addicts, tells me that *marijuana smoking is a true addiction.*

Because each joint contains different chemicals, including the ten psycho-tropics, it is very difficult for marijuana smokers to define when they are high.

Sometimes they smoke a joint that makes them laugh. Some others smoke joints that gives them "the munchies," so they eat a lot. Some others feel relaxed, and some lose coordination and become confused.

But again, this addiction is very peculiar because of the very different content of different chemicals in each joint.

One stoner might say, "Marijuana is an antidepressant." Another might say, "It helps me to sleep," and a few would say, "It makes me feel on top of the world," but some others might also have acute paranoid reactions. Why are there so many different opinions? Because each joint contains different amounts of the terpenes and the three types of psychotropics:

- Delta 8 and Delta 9 THC are mild psychedelics.
- Cannabidiol and cannabichromine are sedatives.
- Cannabisativine, dehydrocannavisativine, and hordenine are stimulants.

So we have three choices, and since each joint contains different amounts of the psychotropics, the result is quite confusing to many.

The hundreds of terpenes induce effects similar to smelling gasoline fumes or glues, and again, there are many different terpenes in each joint.

Treatments Available for Marijuana Addicts: The Good News

The good news is that marijuana smoking does *not* produce brain damage, and the four hundred chemicals contained in this herb produce long-acting effects that can disappear six months after stopping marijuana smoking.

I have been a physician and a psychiatrist for over forty years, and so I have diagnosed and treated thousands of patients suffering from drug addictions and mental illnesses, and this is the good news for marijuana smokers. Just quit, and you will be a different person in six months. Your mind will be clear, your productivity at work will improve, and you will be able to have children if the marijuana was inducing infertility. All are good news.

The withdrawal symptoms are so mild that they usually do not require prescription medications to tolerate. However, if the anxiety or depression is painful, we have good medications that can help in these cases.

CHAPTER 4

Why Marijuana Is an Illegal Intoxicant

I n the last decade, there have been fantasies of many marijuana addicts that marijuana should be legal. This does not surprise us. Any drug addict would prefer to use his or her drugs and not have any legal consequences. There are thousands or maybe millions of people who have been arrested or incarcerated for smoking marijuana, so we have such a large epidemic that millions of marijuana addicts have tried to legalize it.

The states of Colorado and Washington have passed bills legalizing marijuana, but these legalizations are *illegal in the world*. There is an international law and agreement signed in 1967 at the official meeting of the World Health Organization, and it is still valid. This convention was signed by the presidents and prime ministers of all countries that belong to the World Health Organization. Since 1967, there have been some additions to the list of illegal drugs, but not any deletions.

So I believe it is a fantasy of marijuana smokers (addicts) that they can smoke their drug as a recreational intoxicant, the way we in Western civilizations drink alcoholic beverages. This just is not so. Marijuana cannot be legalized in a town or a state, but the WHO is a serious international organization, one that decides which drugs are legal and which are illegal.

CHAPTER 5

Escalation from Marijuana Smoking to Other Illegal Drugs

t is well known and has been proved in many scientific studies that people addicted to marijuana "escalate" to using other illegal drugs like heroin, cocaine, and amphetamines.

Recently, we have seen an epidemic of heroin addiction, and most of these new heroin addicts continue to smoke marijuana. It is like their second drug addiction. Of course, many of the heroin addicts escalated from marijuana smoking, and many others escalated by first using prescribed opioids like Vicodin and Oxycontin.

The availability in America of amphetamines like methedrine and prescribed pills like Adderall and dextroamphetamines has also produced innumerable cases of escalation from marijuana to amphetamines. The latter addiction is the only one that produces irreversible bran changes in the dopaminergic system of the brain, inducing a psychosis identical to paranoid schizophrenia.

The stoners who can afford it also escalate to cocaine, which is also prevalent but still much more expensive than marijuana, amphetamines, or opioids.

Many of the stoners claim that this is a fallacy, but it has been proved scientifically even in rats. When rats addicted to marijuana smoke are compared to rats who were never exposed to marijuana, if opioids like heroin are available to them, the rats who smoked marijuana also become addicted to heroin. This did not happen in the rats who were not exposed to marijuana.

Which of the stoners go for the heroin, and which go for the stimulants? That depends on the "preference" of the stoner for the sedative or stimulant effect they receive when they smoke their marijuana. As said before, *each joint is different*. Some contain more stimulants, some more sedatives, and some more psychedelics.

Let's emphasize that *marijuana is not a "single" drug*. Marijuana pollutes the brains of users with hundreds of chemicals, ten of which are so far identified as psychotropics, meaning that they have depressant or sedative effects, stimulant effects, or psychedelic effects. And all of these are in addition to the hundreds of terpenes available in any joint of marijuana.

Marijuana smoking is a more complex phenomenon than other single-drug addictions. Stoners are subjected to multiple chemicals in their brains.

One stoner says marijuana makes him sleep better, another just smokes it to get high, and some others smoke to forget their problems. But as with any chemical dependence, this constitutes an addiction. And again, some stoners smoke it daily, some every other day, some weekly, and also many are now eating brownies that contain baked marijuana, which has a much more delayed effect than the smoked marijuana. But still, all are stoners.

CHAPTER 6

Marijuana-Induced Psychoses

Since the nineteenth century, marijuana (or hashish), was known as a drug that can induce psychosis—what are nowadays classified as schizophrenias or psychotic bipolar disorder. In 1864 a master publication came out that is now translated into English by Columbia University, New York, as "Hashish and Mental Alienation." In French the title was published as "Du hashish et de l'alienation mentale," by Joseph Moreau de Tours.

Moreau de Tours and several of his colleagues in Paris had learned from the French troops occupying North Africa of the interesting effects of smoking hashish, so he wanted to reproduce in himself the effects of smoking marijuana. What happened is that he reproduced an acute mental illness that is now recognized as bipolar disorder, manic.

In the last ten to twelve years, the number of scientific publications is large, and it has been described as a schizophreniform psychosis. Some papers just define earlier and more frequent onset of schizophrenias in the population of marijuana smokers.

We had known for years that true genetically predisposed schizophrenics got worse when smoking marijuana, but now the consensus among psychiatrists is that marijuana smoking induces a psychosis that can be diagnosed as schizophrenia. Nowadays we know that a high percentage of young people smoking marijuana develop schizophrenia or psychotic bipolar disorders.

There are at least twenty new scientific papers showing the high incidence of schizophrenia in populations of young pot smokers, even in families who do not have the genetics for this illness. Years ago, we thought that only those who were part of a family with a history of schizophrenia and psychotic bipolar disorder could get sick while smoking marijuana. Now, as stated previously, we know that *anyone smoking marijuana can develop a psychotic disorder.*

CHAPTER 7

The Hoax of Medical Marijuana

O ne of the excuses for smoking marijuana nowadays is that "marijuana is a medicine." *This is completely false. Marijuana is not a medication and cannot be a treatment for any human disease.*

Although it is possible that, one day, one or several of the chemical compounds isolated from marijuana could be synthetized and studied to treat medical problems, the whole herb smoked, containing more than four hundred chemicals, *cannot be smoked as a "medicine."*

Recently a paper has been published showing that cannabidiol (one of the sedative psychotropics in marijuana), can be used to treat some epileptic patients. The results are still controversial.

Marijuana is not useful in treating glaucoma, as stated by the American Society of Ophthalmology.

Marijuana does not help patients with multiple sclerosis, and this has been confirmed by the American Neurological Society.

Marijuana is not a good hypnotic. It just has three sedatives that some people interpret as helping them to sleep.

Marijuana is not an antidepressant, even if being stoned is interpreted by many marijuana smokers as "being happier when smoking or eating marijuana."

So, in summary, marijuana as a medicine is a hoax—an excuse of the marijuana drug dealers to legalize their business of selling marijuana in the so-called "dispensaries." This is just a new class of drug dealers paid in cash by stoners.

CHAPTER 8

Stoners Look for a Psychedelic Effect by Smoking Marijuana

Although we found some scientific studies proving that extremely high doses of THC could have the effects of micrograms of LSD, just smoking one or even ten joints of marijuana *will definitely not produce the effects of LSD nor any good psychedelic.*

There was a very interesting double-blind study done in Lexington, Kentucky, years ago. Half of the volunteers received capsules containing five thousand milligrams of THC, and half of the volunteers received identical capsules with sixty micrograms of LSD.

The result was that they could not differentiate which one was not a psychedelic.

LSD is the most potent of all psychotropics, and it is active at the amazingly low dose of one microgram per kilogram of body mass—that is, one thousandth of one milligram per kilogram of body mass. LSD is an amazing drug! But LSD is not the safest psychedelic.

An important example is the medical student at Harvard Medical School who died after ingesting a dose of LSD given at one time by a professor of psychology named Timothy Leary. This student ran out of the lab where he was given the LSD, screaming that he was Jesus Christ and could do anything. Then he jumped in front of a truck with his hand extended and said, "Stop! I am Jesus Christ!" Unfortunately, he was dead on the scene, and Dr. Leary was fired from Harvard.

The safest psychedelic is psilocybin, extracted from hallucinogenic mushrooms, and later synthetized by Sandoz Laboratories (now Novartis). In the early 1960s, it was available for clinical research, and then the FDA classified it as Type I drug, not for medical use. It has continued to be studied in Europe by German psychiatrists, and it was found to be safe and useful in the treatment of obsessive-compulsive disorders. It also facilitates psychotherapy in difficult cases of personality disorders.

If any of our millions of marijuana smokers are looking for a psychedelic effect, I must assure you that smoking pot is not the answer. It has four hundred chemicals, and with fifteen milligrams of psilocybin, you can have a real psychedelic experience, have visual hallucinations, and so on. You could also try eating fourteen pairs of the hallucinogenic mushroom available in your region of the world. But here is a good example of how one simple chemical like psilocybin can induce a great psychedelic experience, and the combination of the four hundred chemicals in marijuana would not do that.

I am not "recommending" that Americans use psychedelics. I am just saying that if someone wants to have a psychedelic experience, smoking marijuana is not the way to do it—and again, the only safe psychedelic is psilocybin.

CHAPTER 9

Marijuana and Alcohol in America

One of the arguments used by the mass media, such as Bill Maher on HBO, to support legalizing marijuana is that alcohol is worse than marijuana. They are two totally different entities. Marijuana is an herb that is smoked or eaten in brownies, and alcohol includes beverages such as beer, wine, and liquor that have been used for thousands of years in the Western world.

Since many Americans descend from a European culture, for them, alcohol drinking in the form of wine, beer, and liquor is an old cultural intoxicant.

Marijuana or the concentrated form, hashish, has been used culturally only by the Muslims. In the old Arab world, hashish smoking is really cultural, but it is not a cultural habit in America, which is 100 percent of European origins (English, Scottish, Irish, French, German, Italian, Scandinavian, and so on).

Alcohol is also addictive—there's no question about that—but almost everyone in America drinks alcohol, and we have about five million alcoholics (ill people), while not many millions have tried marijuana, and we already have over twenty million marijuana addicts. The main thing is that alcohol, again, is one chemical—ethanol—and marijuana is a combination of more than four hundred chemicals polluting the brain.

Alcohol is often drunk with meals, while marijuana induces the "munchies." Alcohol helps digestion of foods; marijuana does not. Most people who drink beer, wine, or liquor have a "palate" for their flavors, and only when drunk in large amounts does alcohol induce intoxication.

Alcohol is metabolized (broken down in the liver) in approximately eight to twelve hours, but marijuana chemicals stay in your brain for months after smoking one joint. As you can see, they are very different, and in terms of damage to society, marijuana induces many more problems than alcohol.

Lately it has been proven that most automobile accidents are induced by intoxication with marijuana and opioids, *not by alcohol*. So marijuana impairs drivers more than alcoholic beverages do.

CHAPTER 10

Mass Killings in America in the Last Decade

The first mass killing happened in Columbine High School in Colorado, and it was well known that the two killers were marijuana addicts. But the mass media does not mention that. They always claim they were "mental cases." Then the killer at a theater in Aurora, Colorado, was also a pothead, and again, not even in his trial was it mentioned that he was always intoxicated with marijuana.

Then came the horrible killing in Tucson, where US congresswoman Gabrielle Giffords was shot in the head, and several others died. This was also perpetrated by a psychotic young man, *but his psychosis was produced by his chronic marijuana smoking.*

Then we have the sick young man who killed his mother and then went to Sandy Hook Elementary School and murdered many children. He was a marijuana addict. And again, the mass media never mentions the marijuana as a problem in these horrible mass murders.

The South Korean guy who killed thirty-two students and injured seventeen others on the Virginia Tech campus was also a marijuana smoker.

The young blond guy who killed nine black people at a church in South Carolina was a pothead too. He is still awaiting trial. I hope this time the media mentions his marijuana smoking; now they only describe him as a racist.

The most recent mass killing happened at a junior college in Oregon. I am still awaiting the autopsy report, which I hope will be published. I am almost sure they will find marijuana in his body.

Also recently, a marijuana addict killed his wife and child and then killed himself.

CHAPTER 11

Conclusion

The purpose of this book is to INFORM ALL MARIJUANA SMOKERS of all the scientific facts on the effects of marijuana in polluting your brains. If you desire to continue smoking this herb, you, at least should know what chemicals you are introducing to your brain, and the many deleterious effects this action has.

Remember that marijuana contains 10 psychotropics : THC as a psychedelic, cnnabidiol as a sedative, three stimulants (hordenine, cannabisativine and dehydrocannabisativine,) but also marijuana contains 400 chemicals more, that are long chain hydrocarbons (like gasoline fumes or glues) and these also you are smoking them introducing them to your brains.

Even if you do not know it now, you might later escalate to other drugs like opioids, cocaine and amphetamines (like methedrine), once your brain "talks to you" and decides marijuana is too weak, and needs more potent drugs to use.

Also, please remember the bad news and the good news. BAD NEWS you might become schizophrenic or bipolar psychotic, at least very paranoid, and escalate to other drugs that might kill you.

THE GOOD NEWS Marijuana smoking does not produce irreversible brain changes like amphetamines do, so if you decide to quit smoking marijuana, in about six months your brain will be TOTALLY FREE, functioning normally and you will have again a clear mind, and no memory problems.

Jose Carranza, M.D.